Introduction for Parents and Professionals

Once children have begun to understand what it means to have an attention disorder and take steps to positively influence their own lives, they benefit from the opportunity to try ideas on their own and thus develop a repertoire of behaviors that work for them at home and school. This *Activity Book* introduces a wide range of suggestions that can be used to gain mastery over some of the more difficult aspects of AD/HD: distractibility, impulsivity, poor planning skills, lack of organization, and a sense of isolation from peers. As children learn to deal with each of these problems in a positive way, their control over their lives is increased. This new edition reflects the many recent developments in the ever-changing field of AD/HD management. As parents and professionals learn more about the disorder, new ways to help children cope have been introduced. We have provided more activities that reflect current developments, such as the importance of exercising and using green space. Over the years, we have enjoyed the feedback we have received from parents, counselors and therapists who have shared with us how children have used the *Activity Book* in a variety of settings. That has inspired us to incorporate additional material that will be helpful and enjoyable to our readers.

The structure of this *Activity Book* allows it to be used in a variety of ways. While many of the pages can be done independently, others lend themselves to collaborative work with an adult who is significantly involved in the young person's life: a parent, grandparent, counselor, or teacher. Working together with an adult provides an opportunity for discussion of various issues: why a strategy worked or did not, how an adult finds a similar activity relevant in her or his life, or how problems affect one's self-image.

Most pages can be done in any order. Kids should not be expected to do many activities at one time. The goal is to make trying new approaches a pleasant experience. Some of the pages are specifically identified as ones to be copied so they can be used repeatedly. Other pages present the activity once, but could easily be expanded by a parent, teacher, or counselor. Kids may enjoy modifying some of the activity pages on their own computer. They might also enjoy trying the same activities at different times (such as the beginning of the school year, then at the end). This may help them see how they have changed.

This Activity Book serves as a companion to our book, *Putting on the Brakes, Third Edition: Understanding and Taking Control of Your ADD or ADHD*. In this book, characteristics of attention deficit hyperactivity disorder were described and young people were offered specific techniques for gaining control. The overwhelming, positive response to our book gave a clear message: Young people welcome the chance to get to know themselves better when the format is respectful, clear and relevant. The adults in their lives are also grateful for a tool that facilitates communication and encourages children's attempts to take responsibility for their own behavior and growth in practical ways. Along with the message that attention deficit disorder brings its unique set of problems, comes the clear statement that there are abundant solutions to be tried. In the *Activity Book* children will be shown new strategies and encouraged to develop even more on their own. Young people learn by doing and by evaluating their successes and mistakes. Working in this *Activity Book* will enable a child to practice many of the concepts presented in *Putting on the Brakes* in a way that is fun and developmentally appropriate.

We have attempted to address the issues that children, parents, counselors and teachers have identified as particularly problematic in dealing with AD/HD. Approaching these issues from our combined backgrounds in pediatrics and education has encouraged us to look at the varied ways children with AD/HD can become involved with understanding AD/HD, making improvements, and having fun in the process.

—Patricia O. Quinn, MD
Developmental Pediatrician

—Judith M. Stern, MA
Learning Specialist

Table of Contents

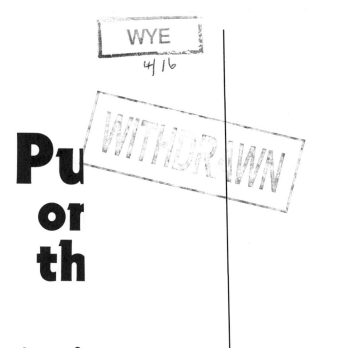

Pu
or
th

Acti

es

r ADHD

econd Edition

by Patricia O. Quinn, MD
and Judith M. Stern, MA

illustrated by Joe Lee

Magination Press • Washington, DC
American Psychological Association

Figure C on page 64 reprinted with permission from *Can You Believe Your Eyes? Over 250 Illusions and Other Visual Oddities* by J. Richard Block and Harold Yuker (Taylor and Francis, 1989)

Published by
MAGINATION PRESS
An Educational Publishing Foundation Book
American Psychological Association
750 First Street, NE
Washington, DC 20002

For more information about our books, including a complete catalog, please write to us,
call 1-800-374-2721, or visit our website at www.maginationpress.com.

Printed by Worzalla, Stevens Point, Wisconsin

Library of Congress Cataloging-in-Publication Data

Quinn, Patricia O.
Putting on the Brakes activity book for kids with ADD or ADHD / by Patricia O. Quinn and Judith M.
Stern ; illustrated by Joe Lee. — 2nd ed.
p. cm.

Earlier ed. entered under title.
Rev. ed. of: The "best of Brakes" activity book for kids with ADD and ADHD.
Includes bibliographical references and index.

ISBN-13: 978-1-4338-0441-0 (pbk. : alk. paper)
ISBN-10: 1-4338-0441-7 (pbk. : alk. paper) 1. Attention-deficit-disordered children—Education
(Elementary)—Juvenile literature. 2. Attention-deficit-disordered children—Recreation—Juvenile
literature. 3. Hyperactive children—Recreation—Juvenile literature. 4. Creative activities and seat
work—Juvenile literature. I. Stern, Judith M. II. Breaks (Magination Press) III. "Best of Brakes" activity
book for kids with ADD and ADHD. IV. Title.

LC4713.2.B48 2009

371.93--dc22

2008050570

10 9 8 7 6 5 4

How to Use This Book

To the boys and girls who use this book:

It's not easy having either ADD or ADHD. (In this book, we refer to both by using AD/HD.) It takes a lot of hard work and practice to learn to manage AD/HD. We have both worked with many kids with AD/HD. We've watched them use these techniques and ideas to solve problems and manage their AD/HD. Lots of kids we know with AD/HD are full of wonderful ideas. As you use this book, you may come up with other good suggestions.

This *Activity Book* contains ideas and suggestions that will help you manage your AD/HD. It's filled with information on

- managing attention problems
- medication
- self-control
- homework
- planning
- organization
- concentration
- and so much more!

We hope that this book will also help you to understand yourself better. Have fun with these activities!

This book might be me more enjoyable if you complete just a few pages at a time. If you like, you can do the activities in any order. As you go through the book, you'll notice that the arrow icon points out the directions for the activities and the light bulb icon indicates extra tips for you. If you come across a word that you do not understand while working in the book, check the glossary on pages 93 and 94 where you can look up the word yourself. If you need help with an activity or want to talk about any of them, be sure to let someone know. People such as your parents teachers, tutor, therapist, or counselor are there to help you when you need it.

Remember, your AD/HD is just one part of you. Try hard to manage it, and you'll have plenty of energy left over to enjoy the many other parts of life as well. This book will help you get started!

Patricia O. Quinn, MD
Judith M. Stern, MA

All about AD/HD

What Is AD/HD?

Attention Deficit Hyperactivity Disorder, or AD/HD, is a condition that occurs in about 8 to 12% of all kids in elementary, middle, and high schools. That means that in your school you might find 1 or 2 kids who have a problem paying attention in each class. AD/HD affects girls and boys around the world. As many as 4 million kids in the United States may have AD/HD.

AD/HD can cause kids to have problems at school and at home. Kids with AD/HD have a hard time paying attention, focusing, listening, and remembering. Some kids with AD/HD have trouble learning, finishing what they start, or keeping track of things. Kids with AD/HD can also have problems getting along with their brothers and sisters or making and keeping friends.

The main problem behaviors (symptoms) of AD/HD are:

Distractibility having difficulty focusing on just one thing

Inattentiveness having trouble paying attention

Impulsivity acting without thinking

Hyperactivity having trouble keeping still

 Not all kids with AD/HD have problems in every area. The checklist on page 15 will help you to take a look at these areas and decide which ones best describe you.

What Part of the Body Controls Attention?

Scientists have found that AD/HD is caused by problems with chemical messengers in your brain called neurotransmitters that send messages from one cell (neuron) in the brain to another. Messages to put on the brakes, slow down, and pay attention may not be getting through as well as they should. The good news is that AD/HD does not affect the parts of the brain that involve intelligence. Kids with AD/HD are just as smart as other kids.

 Label the picture of the brain below. If you want, you can go ahead and color it, too. Use the model below to help you.

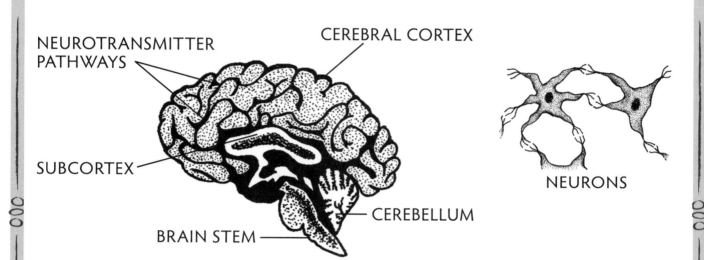

NEUROTRANSMITTER PATHWAYS

CEREBRAL CORTEX

SUBCORTEX

NEURONS

CEREBELLUM

BRAIN STEM

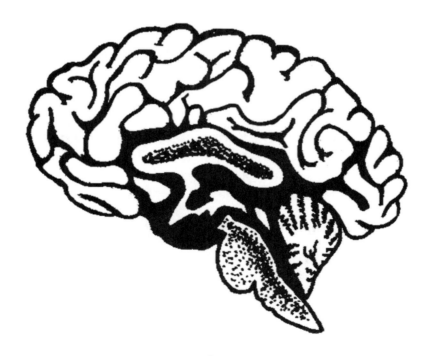

AD/HD Symptom Detective

Let's take a closer look at each of the symptoms of AD/HD described on page 10. Pick the situations that best describe each symptom. Have any of these ever happened to you?

➡️ **Put an X before each example that correctly describes a symptom of AD/HD. There may be more than one answer in some of the examples. If the same situation has happened to you, put a circle around the X.**

Distractibility

☐ Every time other kids are talking outside in the hallway at school, David pays attention to them rather than his classwork.

☐ Elena has problems doing her homework in the family room where her brother is watching TV.

☐ Tracy can concentrate on her science project for hours, even though there's a bird's nest right outside her window.

Inattentiveness

☐ When reading a book, Stuart can focus for only about 5 minutes before he loses his place.

☐ Judy can work on a jigsaw puzzle for over an hour without stopping.

☐ Lang often does not know what he has to do for homework because he was not listening to the teacher.

Impulsivity

☐ Ari knows the rules about walking at the pool, but often can't stop himself from running.

☐ Susie always asks permission before she rides her bike to the playground.

☐ Carlos sometimes gets into trouble for yelling out the answer in class without raising his hand.

Hyperactivity

☐ Patrick can sit through his family's dinner without getting up from the table.

☐ Jesse often taps his pencil on his desk and jiggles his legs while sitting in class.

☐ Padma has trouble when watching a movie. She squirms and moves a lot, often putting her feet all over the furniture or on other people. No one wants to sit near her.

Solving AD/HD Problems

The symptoms of AD/HD (inattentiveness, distractibility, impulsivity, and hyperactivity) often cause problems for kids with AD/HD. Thinking about a problem and trying out some solutions can help change a behavior. It can also be helpful to talk over problems with adults, like counselors or your parents. This page will help you practice finding solutions to problems caused by AD/HD.

 Read each of the problem situations presented below. Check the solution or solutions you think will be best for making each situation better. Write your own solutions on the blank lines provided for you after each story.

1. Sandy was sitting in her classroom before class began. Her good friend, Ada, walked into the room with a new haircut that Sandy did not like. Sandy should:

   ☐ Immediately say that Ada has an ugly haircut.

   ☐ Not make any comments until Ada has asked her opinion.

   ☐ Keep her opinion to herself.

   Other ideas _____

2. Joe has a hard time paying attention to his science teacher. What do you think might be helpful for Joe to do while his teacher is talking?

   ☐ Avoid sitting next to his friend.

   ☐ Read a science book.

   ☐ Try harder to look at the teacher while she's talking.

   ☐ Try taking notes on important things that the teacher says.

   ☐ Close his eyes while listening.

   Other ideas _____

3. Your cousin seems to lose things all the time. Which of these suggestions would you make to her?

   ☐ Set up her room with specific places to put things.

   ☐ Carry important supplies around with her at all times.

   ☐ Clean her backpack out at least once a week.

   ☐ Keep a box in a special place at home for storing school materials.

   Other ideas _____

4. Abdul has problems getting his homework done and handed in on time. Which of the following suggestions might help him?

☐ Set up an after-school schedule to get work done.

☐ Work in a quiet space without distractions.

☐ Leave his homework on the desk in his room when he is finished.

☐ Ask his mom to sit near him so he stays on track.

☐ Only watch TV as a reward if he has all his work done.

Other ideas _____

5. Jessie often can't sit still. What can she do to help herself when she has to sit for a long time?

☐ Get plenty of exercise before she has to sit down.

☐ Walk around the room without asking permission.

☐ Make sure she has a comfortable seat with plenty of room for her to stretch out.

☐ Use a fidget tool (like a small squeeze ball) to help her pay attention.

Other ideas _____

6. José does his homework almost every night but can't find it the next day when the teacher tells everyone to hand it in. He could try:

☐ Carrying it in his hand when he goes to school.

☐ As soon as he finishes each assignment in the afternoon, putting it right in a homework folder that he keeps in his backpack.

☐ Putting it on the kitchen table and trying to remember to take it in the morning.

☐ Putting it in the correct subject section of his notebook so it is easy to find.

Other ideas _____

7. Mei likes to draw when she comes home from school. Sometimes she starts her homework late and doesn't get to finish it before she has to go to sleep. Which of these might work for her?

☐ Doing homework first, then spend free time drawing.

☐ Throwing away her drawing supplies.

☐ Watching more television.

☐ Making a schedule when she gets home. Write in when she will do her work and when she will draw. Write in her bedtime also.

Other ideas _____

AD/HD Checklist

AD/HD cannot be cured, but there are lots of things you and your parents and teachers can do to make your AD/HD symptoms better. You will see many of these suggestions in this book. First, let's take a look at some of your own problems with AD/HD.

It is important to know how AD/HD affects you. Knowing what is difficult for you will help you come up with plans to work on these challenges.

Let's try to identify some of your problems with AD/HD.

 Put a check next to any of the sentences below that describe you or your behavior.

- ☐ It's hard for me to pay attention when my teachers or parents are talking to me.

- ☐ When I should be working, my mind wanders.

- ☐ I have trouble starting my work.

- ☐ I have trouble finishing my work.

- ☐ I do things without thinking first.

- ☐ I am disorganized.

- ☐ I have trouble sitting still.

- ☐ I have trouble making or keeping friends.

- ☐ I have trouble following rules.

- ☐ I forget what I am supposed to do.

- ☐ It's hard for me to get ready for school on time in the morning.

- ☐ Noises or other children in the classroom distract me.

- ☐ I frequently lose things.

 Once you have finished this page, review it with your parent, teacher, or counselor. Together, you can talk about ideas to work on some of these areas. Try to come up with some of your own ideas. You'll also see that this book contains a lot of suggestions that may help.

What I've Learned about AD/HD

Here is a page for you to fill in whenever you learn something new about AD/HD or find a suggestion that helps you manage your AD/HD better. Look for suggestions in this and other books about AD/HD. Your teacher, tutors, counselors, or parents may also have good ideas that you might want to write here.

1 _____

2 _____

3 _____

4 _____

5 _____

6 _____

7 _____

8 _____

9 _____

10 _____

All about You

All kids with AD/HD have good qualities they can be proud of. This section of the book will help you get to know yourself and appreciate your many good qualities.

It is important to learn as much as you can about yourself, as well as about AD/HD. As you grow up, taking time to look at your feelings and what is difficult for you will help you be successful in school and afterwards.

What Are You Like?

Which of the following sentences describe you? This exercise will help you remember your good and interesting qualities. They are a very important part of who you are, and people appreciate these parts of you!

 Put a check next to the ones that describe you. You can describe yourself in your own words at the end.

☐ I am full of energy.

☐ I have lots of good ideas for having fun.

☐ I am good at sports.

☐ I am funny and make people laugh.

☐ I like to build things and work on creative activities.

☐ I am kind to my family and kids at school.

☐ I am a good friend.

☐ I like to help others.

☐ I like adventures.

☐ I am good with animals.

☐ I am a good problem solver.

☐ I have a great imagination.

☐ I am smart.

☐ I am a good reader.

☐ I am good at art.

☐ I am good at math.

I am _____

_____

_____

I like _____

_____

_____

How Do You Feel?

Kids with AD/HD have all kinds of feelings.

 Circle the feelings that you have sometimes.

At the bottom of the page, there is room for you to add other feelings you have had. When you are finished, you can share this page with your parents or counselor so that they can learn more about you.

Angry	Special	Proud
Energetic	Artistic	Popular
Creative	Worried	Afraid
Sensitive	Enthusiastic	Funny
Hyper	Curious	Lonely
Smart	Strong	Disorganized
Picked on	Frustrated	Tense
Friendly	Misunderstood	Determined
Impatient	Good looking	Confused
Stupid	Forgetful	Happy

_____ _____ _____

_____ _____ _____

_____ _____ _____

_____ _____ _____

You Are a Wonderful Person

Here's your chance to see how amazing people think you are. Take some time to ask your parents, a friend, and a teacher to write down something they think is great about you. When this page is full, copy it and hang it over your desk or bed so you can look at it to see how special and appreciated you are.

My parents say that I am:

_____

_____

_____

My teacher says:

_____

_____

_____

My friend says:

_____

_____

_____

The best things about me by ME:

_____

_____

_____

 You can also make your own page so that you can ask more people to talk about you. You could talk to anyone who is important to you, like your grandparent, cousin, coach, or neighbor. You could use the pads that reporters have and interview these people.

Me and My AD/HD

AD/HD causes problems with paying attention. However, there are things that you and others (your parents, teachers, or friends) can do to help you pay better attention. Complete the following sentences to learn more about you and your AD/HD. When you are finished, you can share these ideas with an adult or a group of other kids with AD/HD. The people you share this page with will learn many important things about you.

———○C○○———

Paying Attention

I have a hard time paying attention when _____

_____

I concentrate best when _____

_____

A good place for me to sit in the classroom is _____

When I am not paying attention, I like my teacher to _____

_____

What I Don't Like to Hear

I don't like it when my mom or dad tells me to _____

I don't like it when my teacher says _____

What I Find Helpful

These things help when I feel like I need to move around or fidget _____

_____

Time out works well for me when _____

I like to talk to _____ because he/she understands me.

What Motivates Me

When I am finished working, I like to _____

More about Me

There are *many* things about you that make you special. Here is a chance for you to talk about yourself. This page can also be shared with someone important to you.

I am very good at _____

This year I have gotten better at _____

My favorite subject in school is _____

The subject I like least is _____

One of the best books I ever read was _____

_____

If I could travel anywhere, I would like to go to _____

When I play with a friend, I like to _____

I like to _____ with my family.

My favorite meal is _____, _____,

and _____.

If I could plan the perfect day, this is what I would want to do in the

morning _____

afternoon _____

evening _____

Something about myself I would like to change is _____

_____

What I like best about myself is _____

_____

Learning from Mistakes

Everyone makes mistakes, but we can always learn from them.

———— ⊙O⊙ ————

➡ **Write a story about a mistake you made that caused a problem or got you into trouble (or both!).**

_____

_____

_____

_____

_____

_____

_____

_____

_____

_____

_____

_____

_____

_____

_____

_____

Write about what you did to make things better.

_____

_____

_____

_____

_____

_____

Did your plan work?   ☐ Yes   ☐ No

If not, why do you think it didn't work?

_____

_____

_____

_____

_____

If not, what would you do differently next time?

_____

_____

_____

_____

_____

part 3

Help Managing Your AD/HD

Lots of things can help you manage your AD/HD better. Getting support from others is important, but there are plenty of things you can do to help yourself. Activities in this section may give you some new ideas.

Building an AD/HD Support Team

There are many people who help kids with AD/HD. Remember, you don't have to deal with your AD/HD alone! Below is a list of some of the people who are part of the team that helps kids with AD/HD.

 See if you can find these team members in the word search below.

PARENT

TEACHER

COUNSELOR

TUTOR

THERAPIST

RELATIVES

DOCTOR

NURSE

FRIEND

COACH

BABYSITTER

PSYCHOLOGIST

S	F	T	R	I	G	W	M	R	L	Q	D	Z	A	U	T	I	J
V	L	Q	Z	V	J	X	B	C	P	U	A	O	W	Q	G	K	P
O	L	B	P	D	E	Y	S	T	J	T	E	A	C	H	E	R	B
R	U	X	A	U	V	I	D	O	L	N	B	H	X	T	U	K	H
J	Z	R	V	B	A	U	R	Z	P	R	G	J	W	F	O	V	E
M	T	E	L	Q	Y	H	G	C	A	C	D	F	N	V	D	R	F
X	G	L	H	D	P	S	N	F	R	I	E	N	D	T	U	W	T
R	V	A	S	X	W	Q	I	M	E	V	X	R	U	N	Z	S	U
S	Z	T	D	N	J	M	J	T	N	M	K	G	X	Q	I	D	T
E	K	I	C	C	R	P	B	Z	T	C	W	V	A	G	R	N	O
B	Y	V	M	O	D	H	R	V	G	E	D	J	O	H	S	C	R
T	H	E	R	A	P	I	S	T	X	Z	R	L	V	K	M	D	H
X	M	S	D	C	V	Q	M	C	Y	V	O	B	C	H	X	Z	F
L	R	A	F	H	B	Y	W	L	B	H	Q	G	E	S	R	U	N
M	H	O	V	B	S	X	R	V	C	E	I	L	C	D	K	A	L
D	B	W	M	Y	F	K	G	Y	V	K	D	N	U	G	S	H	I
Q	Y	H	C	O	U	N	S	E	L	O	R	X	H	F	X	E	H
F	C	X	R	J	A	P	D	C	Q	P	L	B	R	K	T	G	M

Homework Help

Forget to write down one of your assignments?
Have a question about how to do some homework?
Need a friend to study for a test with you?

 Fill in this page and hang it in your room.
Next time you need homework help, you'll know where to go!

homework buddies

Name	Phone Number	E-mail
_____	_____	_____
_____	_____	_____

parents

Work Phone Number	Cell Phone Number	E-mail
_____	_____	_____

tutor

Work Phone Number	Cell Phone Number	E-mail
_____	_____	_____

School's Homework "Hotline" _____

Teacher's School E-mail Address _____

Public Library Information Number _____

Helpful Homework Websites http://www.refdesk.com/homework.html

_____

_____

_____

Eating Healthy

When you eat healthy food, you are treating your body well. A good breakfast and lunch will not only give you energy for your day, but will also help you stay more focused on your work. Don't forget to eat healthy at dinner, too!

An afternoon snack helps many kids with AD/HD feel better when it's time to start homework. Here are some ideas for healthy snacks.

 Circle the snacks you might like to eat when you are hungry.

A bowl of soup

Trail mix or granola

A bowl of spaghetti

A salad

Hummus and pita

A bowl of chili

Crackers and tuna

Bagel and cheese

Cinnamon toast

Nuts

Peanut butter and banana sandwich

Sliced fresh fruit

Cubes of cheese

Yogurt

Frozen grapes or blueberries

Carrot and celery sticks

Peanuts and raisins mixed together

Applesauce

Popcorn

A piece of cold chicken

A big slice of watermelon

Baked potato

Whole grain cereal

Celery with peanut butter

 What are some other healthy snacks that you like? List some other ideas for healthy snacks here.

_____   _____

_____   _____

_____   _____

My Healthy Food List

Now it's your turn to write down the foods that you like and will eat. Talk to your parents about this list. You might even want to put a list like this somewhere in the kitchen. How about hanging it on the refrigerator door so that you can read it when you're looking for something to eat? Be sure to include a variety of foods.

my healthy food list by _____

foods I like for breakfast

_____   _____

_____   _____

_____   _____

foods I like for lunch

_____   _____

_____   _____

_____   _____

foods I like for dinner

_____   _____

_____   _____

_____   _____

foods I like for snacks

_____   _____

_____   _____

_____   _____

Exercise Can Be Fun!

Exercise is important for a healthy body. Scientists have found that exercise can help your mind as well. Regular exercise helps kids with AD/HD feel better, improves their mood, and may make them less hyperactive.

To be effective, exercise needs to get your muscles working and your heart beating faster.

Exercising with your friends can increase the fun. So look for an exercise buddy and GET MOVING!

 From the following list of activities that kids like to do, circle the ones you think give both your muscles and your heart a workout. Underline the ones you would like to try.

Running	Lacrosse
Jumping rope	Basketball
Swimming	Golf
Dancing	Watching TV
Playing the piano	Fishing
Tennis	Biking
Wrestling	Playing catch
Building a snowman	Karate
Soccer	Field hockey
Building models	Flying kites
Playing chess	Doing puzzles

 In the space below, list some other fun activities that will give you a workout that you might like to try.

_____   _____

_____   _____

_____

Playing Outdoors for Exercise

There are lots of ways to get your body moving.

We have listed the items hidden in the list below. How many can you find?

 Take a look at the picture below and find the equipment that you will need to participate in various outdoor activities.

- swim goggles
- tennis racket
- golf club
- soccer ball
- basketball hoop
- badminton birdie
- baseball bat
- lacrosse stick
- roller skates
- skateboard
- skis
- sled
- ice skates
- bicycle
- bowling pin
- football helmet
- running shoes
- hockey stick
- boxing gloves

Your Exercise Log

Adding exercise to your to-do list and your daily schedule is an important way to make sure you get moving. By keeping an exercise log you can be sure to get at least 30 minutes of exercise every day.

Here is a sample log:

MON	Rode bikes with Sam	1.5 hours
TUES	Soccer practice	2 hours
WED	Shot baskets	1 hour
THURS	Walked the dog	20 minutes
FRI	Bowled with my family	2 hours
SAT	Soccer game	1 hour
SUN	Swimming	3 hours

Here is a log for you to fill in for a week:

my exercise log

Day	Activity	Time
MON	_____	_____
TUES	_____	_____
WED	_____	_____
THUR	_____	_____
FRI	_____	_____
SAT	_____	_____
SUN	_____	_____

 If you like keeping track of your weekly exercise, make up a log or copy this page to complete each week. Share this with others to see if they would like to keep their own log as well. Maybe you could make one for the entire family.

Finding Your Green Space

Spending time outdoors can help improve our ability to sit still and focus and gives us a chance to enjoy nature. Some kids like to read or do some of their homework outside in a special, peaceful spot. Being active and playing outdoors can reduce hyperactivity as well.

Think of a place outdoors where you enjoy spending time. It helps if there is some "greenery"—trees and grass—there.

 Unscramble these words to come up with some ideas.

1. krpa _____

2. daybakcr _____

3. pdnglaruoy _____

4. kebi htap _____

5. npdo _____

6. rktac _____

7. drgane _____

8. tranuen arlit _____

9. rmpugnocda _____

10. ozo _____

11. eter sueoh _____

12. botraumre _____

13. rneguheeso _____

14. ctaelhit efdlis _____

 Try to think of your favorite green spaces. Explore your neighborhood with your family to find where you can play outdoors safely.

Recognizing Anger's Warning Signs

Kids with AD/HD sometimes have problems controlling their emotions. They may react to situations too quickly and get angry easily. To manage your anger, it helps to learn the early signs that tell you that you might be getting angry. Once you're aware of the signals, you can calm down before it's too late. Kids who get angry a lot need help tuning into their bodies to notice their own early warning signs.

 Look carefully at the pictures of the kids below. Use their facial expressions and body language to give you clues. Circle the pictures that show kids who look angry. Then check their words to see if you're right.

How Can You Relax When You're Upset?

Many kids have a hard time calming down when they are upset. Here are some good ways that people have found to help them relax.

Check the ones that you have tried.

- ☐ Breathe in and out slowly.

- ☐ Count to 10 slowly.

- ☐ Listen to music in a quiet place.

- ☐ Exercise for 30 minutes.

- ☐ Take a long walk (after you have asked permission).

- ☐ Do yoga.

- ☐ Take a cool shower.

- ☐ Take a long bath.

- ☐ Play with your pet.

- ☐ Go outside and throw a ball.

Collect ideas from other people that you know. You can also think up some activities that work for you. Add them here.

_____   _____

_____   _____

_____   _____

_____   _____

_____   _____

Medication Check-Up

If your DOCTOR decides to prescribe medication to help your AD/HD SYMPTOMS, there are lots of things you will need to know. The most commonly prescribed MEDICINES for AD/HD are called STIMULANTS. These medications can help decrease DISTRACTIBILITY and improve FOCUS.

Be sure you learn the NAME of your MEDICATION, the amount (DOSE) you are taking, and the specific TIME you should take your PILL or PATCH each day. If you have SIDE EFFECTS, such as poor APPETITE, trouble sleeping (INSOMNIA), STOMACHACHE, or HEADACHE, be sure to tell your doctor at your next CHECK-UP.

 Look for the words above that are in CAPITALS in the word search below.

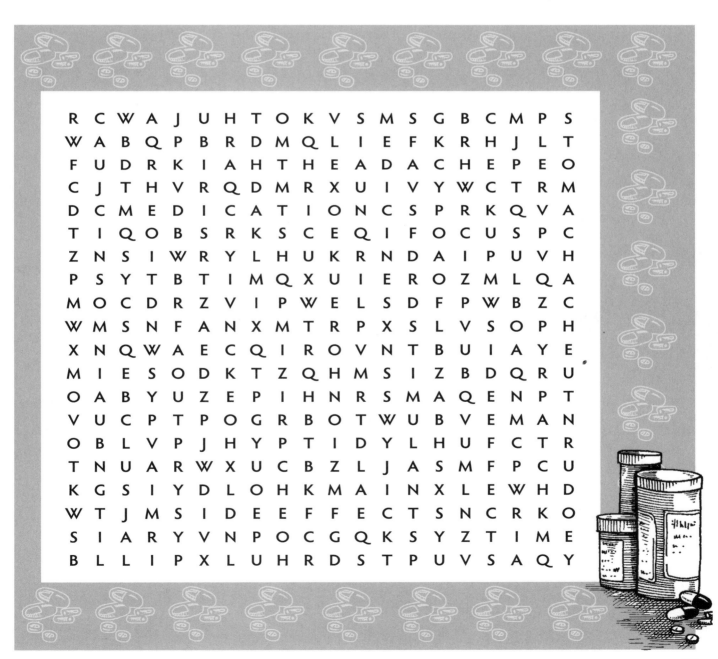

```
R C W A J U H T O K V S M S G B C M P S
W A B Q P B R D M Q L I E F K R H J L T
F U D R K I A H T H E A D A C H E P E O
C J T H V R Q D M R X U I V Y W C T R M
D C M E D I C A T I O N C S P R K Q V A
T I Q O B S R K S C E Q I F O C U S P C
Z N S I W R Y L H U K R N D A I P U V H
P S Y T B T I M Q X U I E R O Z M L Q A
M O C D R Z V I P W E L S D F P W B Z C
W M S N F A N X M T R P X S L V S O P H
X N Q W A E C Q I R O V N T B U I A Y E
M I E S O D K T Z Q H M S I Z B D Q R U
O A B Y U Z E P I H N R S M A Q E N P T
V U C P T P O G R B O T W U B V E M A N
O B L V P J H Y P T I D Y L H U F C T R
T N U A R W X U C B Z L J A S M F P C U
K G S I Y D L O H K M A I N X L E W H D
W T J M S I D E E F F E C T S N C R K O
S I A R Y V N P O C G Q K S Y Z T I M E
B L L I P X L U H R D S T P U V S A Q Y
```

Use the space below to list any questions you might want to ask your doctor at your next check-up.

questions for my doctor

1 _____

_____

2 _____

_____

3 _____

_____

4 _____

_____

5 _____

_____

6 _____

_____

7 _____

_____

Taking Your Medicine

Many kids take medication as part of the treatment for their AD/HD. It helps them pay attention and calm down. If you're one of these kids, use this page together with your parents to help you keep track of when you take your medicine. You can also use it to write down any side effects you want to discuss with your doctor. (Most kids have no side effects from their medication.) Be sure to talk with your parents and doctor if you have questions or concerns about your medicine. If you have any problems with your medicine, your doctor can adjust the dose or change your medication to get the best treatment for you.

 In the form below, put a check mark each time you take a dose as prescribed by your doctor. Be sure to indicate any problems or questions you have during the week.

Name: _____

Week of: _____

Medication name: _____ Dose: _____

Time to be taken: _____a.m. _____p.m. _____p.m.

Monday	_____	_____	_____
Tuesday	_____	_____	_____
Wednesday	_____	_____	_____
Thursday	_____	_____	_____
Friday	_____	_____	_____
Saturday	_____	_____	_____
Sunday	_____	_____	_____

During the week, I had problems with the following:

☐ attention span   ☐ control of behavior   ☐ headaches

☐ distractibility   ☐ sitting still   ☐ stomachaches

☐ completing assignments   ☐ trouble sleeping   ☐ loss of appetite

 You can copy this page so you can use it each week. You can also make your own version on your computer at home.

Setting Your Own Goals

FINISH

Think of something you would like to learn to do. What about something that you could do better? Write your goal here:

_____

_____

_____

_____

Write down the names of people who could help you accomplish this goal:

_____

_____

How long will you try to work on this goal?

☐ one day   ☐ three days   ☐ one week   ☐ two weeks

After that time is up, evaluate yourself.

Did you achieve your goal?

_____

If you were successful, keep up the good work!

If you haven't yet achieved your goal, what could you do to be successful?

_____

_____

_____

How Can You Manage Your AD/HD Better?

Now that you have worked on activities about some of the ways to make your life with AD/HD better, see how many of these questions you can answer. (HINT: All of the answers to these questions can be found in Part 3 of this book.)

 Complete the sentences below by underlining the correct answer from the words in the parenthesis.

1. (Exercising, Getting angry) can help you calm down and relax.

2. Some kids with AD/HD are helped by taking (candy, medicine) to help them pay attention better.

3. Only a (doctor, teacher) can prescribe medicine for AD/HD.

4. When something is bothering you, you (should, should not) talk with someone about it.

5. (Potato chips, An orange) makes a healthy snack.

6. If you don't get enough sleep, it may be harder to (fidget, focus) in school the next day.

7. Cleaning out your backpack (once a week, once a month) makes it easier to stay organized.

8. A (fireman, counselor) should be part of your support team.

9. Listening to music is a good way to (relax, get your homework done).

10. Spending time outdoors in a green space can (increase, decrease) hyperactivity.

11. Exercising (can be, is never) fun.

part 4

Friendships

Friends ....
Share
Laugh
Listen
Play
Help
Encourage
Take turns
Respect
Keep us company

In this section, you will find activities to help you learn what makes a good friend, so you can become one for others.

Making Friends

Making friends is not always easy for kids with AD/HD, but with practice you can learn how to be a good friend to others.

Most friendships come more easily when you choose friends who like the same things that you do. What you choose to do together with your friend can be important!

 Write down 5 things you really like to do. Think of someone you would like to do each of these with.

Here is an example:

I like	This might be fun to do with
Bowling	Jeremy

Now you try it:

I like

This might be fun to do with

1. _____ _____
2. _____ _____
3. _____ _____
4. _____ _____
5. _____ _____

Taking Turns

To be a good friend, you need to be able to take turns when you play games or pick things to do.

Here you will find some suggestions for games and things to do that will help you practice taking turns while you have fun playing with just one other kid. When you get good at it, try playing with two or more kids.

Games to play with One Other Kid

Ping-pong
Hopscotch
Foosball
Tennis
Chess
Checkers
Hangman
Basketball (HORSE)
Pool

Games to Play with Two or More

Write and act out a play
Tetherball
Board games
Card games
Charades
Frisbee
Hide and seek
Freeze tag
Relay races
Put on a talent show

Add your own favorite games here.

_____

_____

_____

_____

_____

_____

_____

Pick a Friend

Take a look at the following situations.

Try to choose the person that you think acted like a good friend.
(HINT: There may be more than one correct answer.)

1. Julie has forgotten her lunch at home. Which girl acted like her friend?

   ☐ Vicki offers to share her lunch with Julie.

   ☐ Susan reminds Julie that she is always forgetting something.

   ☐ Annette tells Julie where she can buy some snacks.

2. Today is Tomás' birthday. Who spoke like a friend?

   ☐ Ritu doesn't mention it.

   ☐ Naoto says, "Happy Birthday" as soon as he sees Tomás coming.

   ☐ Willie asks if Tomas is going to have a party.

3. David and Sean (two big football players) have recently been bullying Joe because he is small and quiet. They make fun of him in front of other kids at the lunch table. Who acted like a friend?

   ☐ Sammi (another football player) asks Joe to come over to his table.

   ☐ Antonio orders Joe to come and throw the table's trash away.

   ☐ Svetla comes over to Joe and asks him to help her with her science project. She tells him that he's the best student in the science class.

4. Tatiana falls on the playground. Who acted like a friend?

   ☐ Ricky laughed at her and called her clumsy.

   ☐ Patty helped her up and brushed her off.

   ☐ Jack got angry at her for interrupting the game.

5. Jasmine and her 6th grade classmates like to say means things about Maddie when she's not there. The other girls usually laugh at what she says. Who acts like a friend?

☐ Rose tells another mean story about Maddie.

☐ Kim says she's not comfortable talking about people behind their back and walks away.

☐ Ricki goes and tells Maddie.

☐ Jami changes the subject and says, "Let's go play soccer."

6. Ben left his homework assignment pad at school. Who acted like a friend?

☐ Michael offered to come over and share his books and assignment sheets.

☐ Justin said he doesn't have time. He was too busy playing with his friends.

☐ Luis read the assignments to Ben over the phone.

7. Sara's dog gets out of the yard where she is playing with her friends. Who acts like a good friend?

☐ Anna says over and over, "Oh, what can we do?"

☐ Jesse helps Sara look for her dog.

☐ Cassie runs home because she is afraid she will get into trouble.

What Would You Do?

Being a good friend involves being able to think about how other people might feel. Here are some situations that friends may find themselves in.

 Choose the solution that shows what a good friend would do.

Often there is more than one good way to handle a situation. Some of these stories may have more than one answer. If you have another good way to solve the situation be sure to add it.

1. At recess you find you sometimes have no one to play with. You could:

   ☐ Bring a ball from home to start a game.

   ☐ Pick a fight.

   ☐ Brag about your new computer.

   ☐ Talk to one or two other kids you like.

   Other ideas _____

2. Lee is always losing his temper with friends. Today he yelled at his good friend, Marcos. What should Lee try the next time he gets upset?

   ☐ Count to 10 and take a deep breath.

   ☐ Walk away and say, "I'm upset now. Let's talk about it later."

   ☐ Cry and scream in front of others.

   Other ideas _____

3. Your good friend and you are playing together in the neighborhood park. A kid from your class comes over and asks if he can join you. You could:

   ☐ Tell your friend you would like to do something together that would be fun with more people (like playing tag).

   ☐ Tell the other kid to go home.

   ☐ Tell your friend to go home.

   ☐ Tell your friend that next time it will be his turn to ask someone to join in.

   Other ideas _____

part 5

Getting Organized

When you're organized, life goes more smoothly.
With practice you can become more organized,
and stay that way, at home and at school.

Organizing Your Room

Keeping organized can help make life easier. When you have specific places to put things, you know where each thing belongs and where you can find it when you need it.

Here's a bedroom that needs some organizing. Take each item that is out of place and put it away.

 Draw a line from each object to where it belongs.

Managing Your Time

Sometimes, it feels like homework will take up your whole evening, or a big project will never get done. There are many ways to manage your time so that you feel more in control. Making a schedule, setting a timer, and using a calendar are all helpful for figuring out how to use the time you have in a good way. Teachers and parents can also help you figure out ways to manage time well, so you don't have to feel like you are always working!

 Fill in your suggestions below.

Don't rush through your work.

Do slow down and work carefully.

Don't try to do a job all at once.

Do _____

_____

Don't leave big projects until the last minute.

Do _____

_____

Don't try to do everything by yourself.

Do _____

_____

Don't start homework too late when you might be tired or run out of time to finish.

Do _____

_____

Packing It Up!

Do you forget to bring everything home you need for homework? Do you sometimes leave things home that you are supposed to bring back to school?

Try making yourself a checklist that you can fill in each day of the week. Write down the things you need to bring home each afternoon. Use another chart that reminds you what you need to pack up each night at home. Some things may always be the same (such as your assignment book), while other items (like a homework worksheet or permission slip) may be different each day.

 Before you leave school, check off each item as you put it in your backpack. You may want to put a clean chart in your notebook or assignment book each week so you're ready to use it each day. You could even make up your own chart at home. If you do, here is a chart you can use as an example.

remember to pack at the end of the school day

MON	TUES	WED	THUR	FRI
_____	_____	_____	_____	_____
_____	_____	_____	_____	_____
_____	_____	_____	_____	_____
_____	_____	_____	_____	_____

Here is an example of a reminder chart to use at home, so that you remember to pack up everything you will need for school the next day. Monday's list has been started for you.

my pack-it-up list for school the next day

MON	TUES	WED	THUR	FRI
Notebook	_____	_____	_____	_____
Pencils	_____	_____	_____	_____
Calculator	_____	_____	_____	_____
Lunch	_____	_____	_____	_____
_____	_____	_____	_____	_____
_____	_____	_____	_____	_____

Making Your Morning Go Smoothly

Spending a few minutes each night organizing for the next day will make your mornings go better. Try to think of everything you might need for school.

 Find things that you might need for school in this hidden picture.

pencils	ruler	backpack	thermos
pen	notebook	gym clothes	books
math book	planner	protractor	school papers
homework	lunch box	compass	calculator

Timing Homework

Learning to manage time can help you figure out how much time you will need to get your homework done. For some kids, timing how long each assignment will take helps them to stay better focused.

Remember, the more you practice estimating the time you need for each kind of assignment, the better you will get at it. Soon you will be able to make a homework schedule for yourself, and be able to guess how much time you need for each subject.

Pick one of your homework assignments for today. Guess how long it will take you to complete it.

 Fill in the form below.

Assignment name: _____

How long do you think it will take to complete this work?

Write your guess here: _____

Have someone time how long it actually takes you.

Write that time here: _____

How close was your guess? _____

Did the work take more or less time than you thought? _____

Why do you think this happened? _____

_____

Try this again with another assignment on another day.

Assignment name: _____

How long do you think it will take? _____

How long did it take? _____

After-School Schedule

A daily schedule can help you plan your after-school time so that you can get everything done and still have free time.

When you get home from school, work out a schedule for the afternoon and evening that will include: homework, studying for tests, reading, chores, snacks and dinner, and special activities for the day. Your parents or another adult can help you with this if you need it. As the year goes on, some kids get good at writing their own schedule.

Don't forget to put in short breaks. You deserve them! And they help you concentrate better.

Use the next page to write down your schedule.

Here is a sample to give you some ideas:

3:30   Home!

4:00   Spelling homework

4:30   Free time

5:15   Math homework

5:45   Read for book report

6:00   Dinner

7:00   Practice trumpet

7:20   Finish homework and pack up for school

8:00   Chores

8:15   Free time

9:00   Get ready for bed

9:30   Bed

Your After-School Plan

Use this page to plan your after-school time.

You might want to review this plan with an adult before you start.

Go ahead and make copies of this page so you can make a schedule for each day of the week. You may also want to enter this information into your PDA, if you have one, or on a calendar program on your computer.

my after-school plan

for _____
(day of the week)

3:00 _____

3:30 _____

4:00 _____

4:30 _____

5:00 _____

5:30 _____

6:00 _____

6:30 _____

7:00 _____

7:30 _____

8:00 _____

8:30 _____

9:00 _____

9:30 _____

10:00 _____

Plan for the Month

As you move into middle school (or if you're already there), you will find it helpful to use a large wall calendar (or a white board) each month to keep track of due dates for projects and reports, dates of tests, and important events you must remember.

You may also want to use your smart phone, tablet or desktop computer to set up a calendar. Instead of relying on your memory you can see everything you need to do right in front of you. This is a great planning tool!

calendar

SUN	MON	TUES	WED	THUR	FRI	SAT
	1 study for science test	2 study for science test	3 science test	4	5 class trip	6
7	8 book report due	9	10	11	12 spelling test	13
14	15 NO SCHOOL	16	17 Jenn's birthday party	18 hand in outline for social studies project	19 spelling test	20
21	22 rough draft of social studies project due	23	24 social studies project due	25 dentist appoinment (2:45)	26 spelling test	27
28	29	30				

Drawing Reminders

Many kids with attention problems find it helpful to draw reminders when someone is giving them oral directions. That way there is something to look back at later if they have forgotten what to do. Here is some practice in drawing the directions.

Your parent tells you to remember to do three things after school: feed the dog, take out the trash, and hang up your coat.

Draw three easy pictures that would remind you of what you need to do when you get home.

Today after school, instead of going straight home, you have a doctor's appointment and baseball practice. Then you are going to your grandmother's house for dinner.

Draw pictures to remind yourself of where to go.

For more practice, ask a parent or one of your friends to give you some directions out loud.

Now try to draw pictures that will remind you what to do.

Writing Reminders

Writing brief notes is another way to help remember what you have to do.

 Pretend your teacher gives you the directions below. Write a short list to remind yourself what to do. Write only a few words and not full sentences.

"For school tomorrow remember to bring: permission slip for the class trip to the museum and money for the trip, your gym shoes and shorts for third period, and your math test, which must be signed at the top by one of your parents."

Write your reminder notes here:

_____   _____

_____   _____

_____   _____

_____   _____

_____

"Don't forget that your biography book report is due tomorrow. It must be in a folder with a cover and a bibliography. Make sure that the title, your name, and the date are written neatly on the cover. When you bring it in, you must put it in the red tray on my desk by 9 o'clock."

Write your notes here:

_____   _____

_____   _____

_____   _____

_____   _____

 Once you feel comfortable taking notes for directions, ask someone to give you some short directions. Take notes on what they said. Next, have that person give you a longer set of directions and see if you can take notes on those.

Making Lists

Lists are helpful for remembering important things. Try this activity.

➤ **Make a list of ten things you want to remember to bring the next time you go on vacation.**

1. _____   6. _____

2. _____   7. _____

3. _____   8. _____

4. _____   9. _____

5. _____   10. _____

➤ **Make a list of five items you usually need to bring to school.**

1. _____   4. _____

2. _____   5. _____

3. _____

You have been asked to help entertain your little cousin while his parents paint their kitchen.

➤ **Make a list of five things you can take to his house that you can use to keep him busy.**

1. _____   4. _____

2. _____   5. _____

3. _____

➤ **Make a list of five things you'd like to do at home the next time you're inside on a rainy day.**

These can be things you do alone or together with other people.

1. _____   4. _____

2. _____   5. _____

3. _____

Working Step-by-Step

Planning something big can be a lot of work. Kids and adults often find this a hard thing to do. What is a good solution? One is to write down the steps you need to follow in order to get the job done. Sometimes the order of the steps is very important too, so pay attention to that when you write it down.

Here's an example:

Pretend you are taking care of a neighbor's dog. Below is a list of what you might be asked to do. If you use a list like this to check off each step as you do it, you will be sure to get everything done.

1. Walk Muffy.
2. Change water in Muffy's bowl.
3. Feed Muffy.
4. Play fetch.

Pretend you are planning a sleepover party for your friends. Your parents have asked you to make a list of what needs to be done to prepare for the party.

 Think of ten steps you would need to take to make it a great event. Try to put the list in order of what you would do first, second, and so on.

1. _____   6. _____

2. _____   7. _____

3. _____   8. _____

4. _____   9. _____

5. _____   10. _____

List five things you need to do every night to get ready for bed. Put them in the order you are supposed to do them.

1. _____   4. _____

2. _____   5. _____

3. _____

Sharpening
Your Skills

To become better at a sport, you need to practice. Practice is important to improve other skills as well. Kids with AD/HD sometimes have difficulty paying attention to details, following directions, finishing assignments, organizing, deciding in what order to complete tasks, or managing time. This next section will help you practice and sharpen these skills.

What Do You See?

Paying attention to small details can be the difference between making a careless mistake on a math test or arriving on the right day for a birthday party. To sharpen your skill of looking at something carefully, we have provided some fun exercises.

 Take a look at each picture below and write down what you see.
Now look again. Can you see something different in the same picture?

A. What is this? Look again.

B. Are the black sides inside or outside?

C. What is this?

D. Which vertical section is longer?

What's Wrong Here?

Finding mistakes takes attention to detail. To find mistakes while editing your written work or checking your math you need to pay attention to small details. The picture below has several mistakes.

 Look carefully and find what is wrong with this picture.

Look Carefully

To be a good reader, it's important to look at words carefully so that you don't mistake them for other words that look very similar. Be sure to look at the beginning, middle, and ending of all words.

Here is an activity to give you some practice looking at words.

 Circle the two words in each row that are the same.
If this seems easy to you, try doing it *quickly* and accurately. It's good practice.

1.	slip	slop	slip	slap
2.	quit	quite	quilt	quit
3.	since	sense	since	science
4.	happier	happiness	happiest	happiest
5.	shingle	single	single	singer
6.	coordinated	coordinator	coordinate	coordinated
7.	were	where	we're	were
8.	choose	chose	cheese	chose
9.	three	there	there	their
10.	hoping	holding	hopping	hopping
11.	flight	fight	fright	flight
12.	heartless	heartfelt	heartfelt	heartburn
13.	hematoid	hematosis	hematoza	hematosis

What's the Correct Order?

Doing things in the correct order or sequence is also very important. Can you imagine…
Putting your boots on after you have gone out into the snow? Putting the toothpaste on
your toothbrush after you've brushed your teeth?

 Put the following events in the right order. Put a 1 in front of the event that happens first, a 2 in front of the next step, and so on.

A
- ☐ Jeff went inside to apologize.
- ☐ Jeff broke a window.
- ☐ Jeff hit the ball in his yard.
- ☐ Jeff picked up the bat.

B
- ☐ Now, I have no money.
- ☐ Next, I bought a new pencil.
- ☐ First, I bought two candy bars.
- ☐ Finally, I bought the tape we wanted.
- ☐ I walked to the store to spend my allowance.

C
- ☐ Ted cooked dinner.
- ☐ Jed put the dishes away.
- ☐ Ned dried the dishes.
- ☐ Ed washed the dishes.
- ☐ Fred set the table.

Following a Recipe

You've been practicing following directions and doing things in the right order. Directions are a part of everyday life. With a lot of tasks it is important to follow steps in the correct order so that what you are doing comes out okay. When you cook, it is important to follow the recipe exactly. You must read the directions carefully, prepare your ingredients ahead of time, and do all steps in the correct order. This helps you make sure the food will come out just right.

 Try this recipe for French toast with the help of an adult.

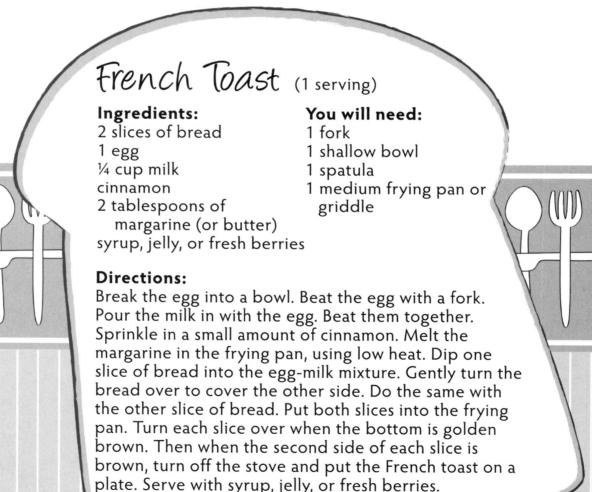

French Toast (1 serving)

Ingredients:
2 slices of bread
1 egg
¼ cup milk
cinnamon
2 tablespoons of
    margarine (or butter)
syrup, jelly, or fresh berries

You will need:
1 fork
1 shallow bowl
1 spatula
1 medium frying pan or
    griddle

Directions:
Break the egg into a bowl. Beat the egg with a fork. Pour the milk in with the egg. Beat them together. Sprinkle in a small amount of cinnamon. Melt the margarine in the frying pan, using low heat. Dip one slice of bread into the egg-milk mixture. Gently turn the bread over to cover the other side. Do the same with the other slice of bread. Put both slices into the frying pan. Turn each slice over when the bottom is golden brown. Then when the second side of each slice is brown, turn off the stove and put the French toast on a plate. Serve with syrup, jelly, or fresh berries.

Try this recipe with the help of an adult.

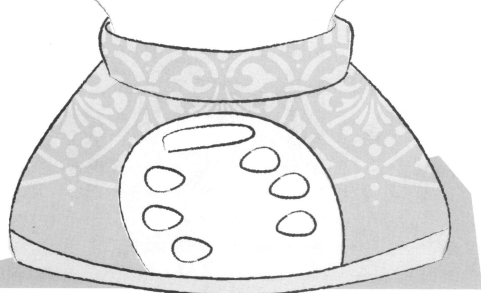

Fruit Smoothie (for 1 person)

Ingredients:
¼ cup of fresh or frozen berries (strawberries,
    raspberries, or blueberries)
1 small banana
4 tablespoons of low-fat vanilla yogurt
1 cup of cold orange juice

You will need: 1 blender
                   1 large glass
                   1 knife

Directions:
1. Cut the banana into four parts.
2. Put all of the fruit into the blender.
3. Add the yogurt and orange juice.
4. Blend all of the ingredients until
   they are smooth.
5. Pour into a large glass and enjoy.

You can make this for more than one person by doubling or tripling the recipe. It will give you a chance to use your multiplication and fraction skills!

Telling the Story

Can you arrange these pictures in the correct order to tell what happened in the story?

 Fill a number in the empty box at the corner of each picture to tell what happens first, second, third, and fourth.

☐

☐

☐

☐

☐

☐

☐

☐

☐

☐

☐

☐

Finish What You Start

An important part of being a successful student is finishing your work. The finished work is what you will be judged on. So for each job you do, start at the beginning and keep at it until you are finished. You will be proud of your completed work and it will give you a skill that you will use throughout your life.

 See if you can stick with the connect-the-dot activity below until it is finished. Don't give up! Keep at it.

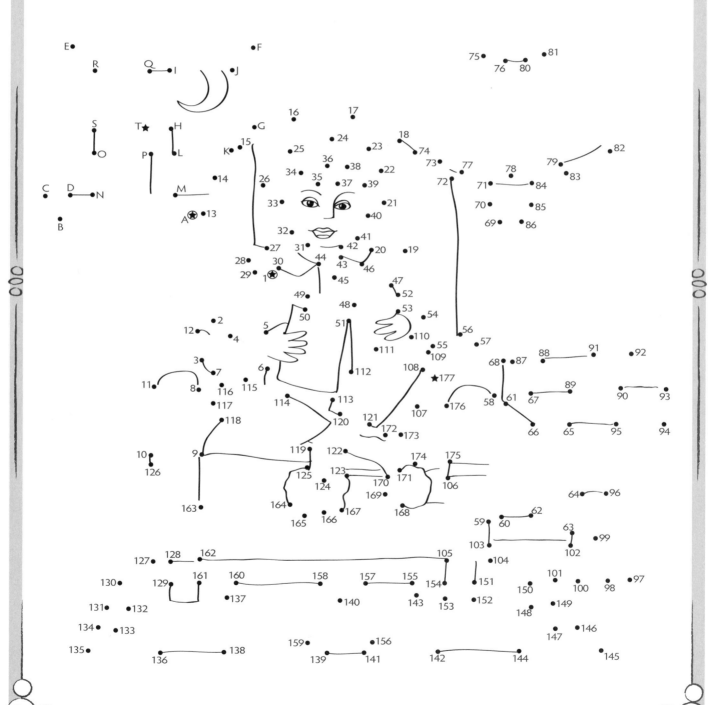

Try It!

Sometimes a task can feel very complicated or look difficult at first. But when you actually get started, you find that it is easier than you thought. After you make an attempt, if you find a task is still too difficult, don't be afraid to ask for help.

 Try working on this maze slowly and carefully. Don't be afraid to ask for help if you need it.

exit   enter

Direction Inspection

When you read directions, it's very important to pay attention to the little words that tell you how to mark your answers. Some "direction words" are: match, circle, connect, cross out, and underline. Many kids find it useful to highlight the special words in directions that explain how to do an assignment. You can highlight by circling, underlining, or using a highlighter marker.

Now let's practice following directions! Be a Direction Inspector.

 Underline the word or words in each sentence that you think are the most important for telling you how to do the exercise.

Example: <u>Put a check next to</u> the best answer.

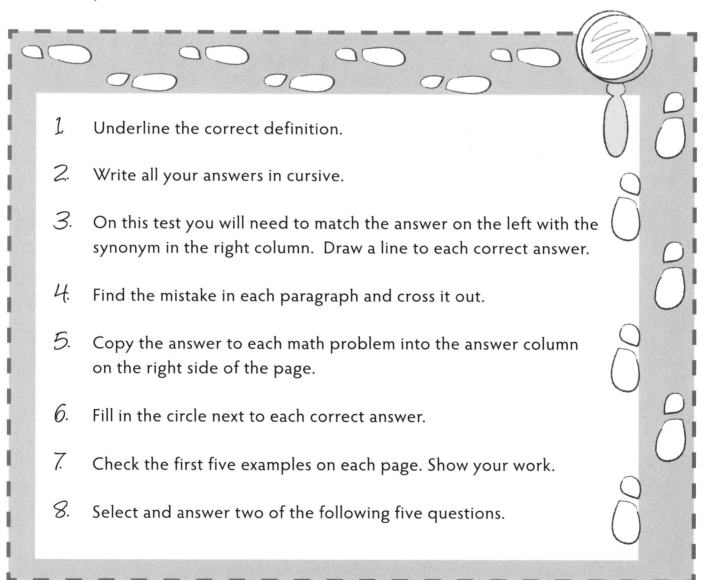

1. Underline the correct definition.

2. Write all your answers in cursive.

3. On this test you will need to match the answer on the left with the synonym in the right column. Draw a line to each correct answer.

4. Find the mistake in each paragraph and cross it out.

5. Copy the answer to each math problem into the answer column on the right side of the page.

6. Fill in the circle next to each correct answer.

7. Check the first five examples on each page. Show your work.

8. Select and answer two of the following five questions.

part 7

Succeeding in School

AD/HD kids are smart but they still might find school to be somewhat difficult. Learning to be organized, managing projects well and checking over work are all important in school and life. In this section, you'll find many ideas and activities to try so that you can improve your skills.

Correcting Your Work

Looking over your work carefully before you hand it in gives you a chance to find mistakes, careless errors and examples you may not have finished. Take the time to look over your work. It can really make a difference!

See if you can do a better job of checking than the person who handed in this paper. How many mistakes can you find on this page of math problems?

 Circle the incorrect answers and see if you can figure out the correct answers.

1. 7 X 9 = 63

2. 4 + 7 = 11

3. 21 + 46 = 66

4. 8 X 6 = 46

5. 3 + 21 = 63

6. 6 X 12 = 64

7. 33 + 22 = 66

8. 9 − 4 = 5

9.
$$
\begin{array}{r}
836 \\
- \ 567 \\
\hline
1403
\end{array}
$$

10.
$$
\begin{array}{r}
560 \\
\times \ 21 \\
\hline
11760
\end{array}
$$

11. 279 ÷ 3 = 93

12.
$$
\begin{array}{r}
2\frac{1}{2} \\
+ \ 7\frac{1}{2} \\
\hline
9\frac{2}{4}
\end{array}
$$

Proofreading Your Work

School assignments need to be done accurately, and that includes finding mistakes and looking carefully when you correct your own work. This skill is called "proof-reading." Remember, everyone makes mistakes. With careful proofreading, you can catch a lot of yours!

Jerry's teacher has a headache. After checking so many papers, he needs a break.

 Look over this assignment that Jerry did. Use a red pen to correct any mistakes he made in punctuation, capitalization, or spelling.

After you're done, walk away for a few minutes. Then come back and look at the page again. Can you find any more mistakes? (You'll find that this is good to do when you're checking over your work, too!)

Last weak we went to visit my ant and uncle, who live in chicago illinois When ant Mary saw me, she said in a loud voice, I cant beleive how much you grown since last year,! We had fun being together Next year, I hop we can spend more then too days in chicago.

Planning Projects

In addition to your daily homework, larger projects will be assigned by your teachers. They expect you to be able to do a little of the work each day. This makes a big assignment easier to manage. When you find out that you have a large project assigned, don't panic and don't avoid the job. Planning will help you get it all done!

You can make large projects easier by making a schedule. Put this schedule into your smart phone, tablet, or desktop computer calendar or on a big wall calendar.

Decide to do part of the project, study for the test, or work on the assignment each day until it is due.

Here is an example of a schedule for a science project:

project schedule

MON	Decide on topic for project.
TUES	Research topic at the library and online.
WED & THUR	Take notes from research.
FRI	Draw diagrams and labels.
SAT	Build project.
MON	Put your project together. Make sure all the directions have followed.
TUES	Project due! Hand it in.

Making a Project Schedule

Spreading out a big task over time is a great strategy. Doing a little at a time, will make a big job feel easier! Making a schedule will help you divide up and plan for a large project. Let's try!

Your friend has a big report to do. She has asked you to help her figure out what she should do each day of the week so she will be done in time. Today is Saturday and the report is due next Friday. She has one week to get everything done.

Here is her project assignment:

Read pages 42-60 in the book about the presidents. Write one page about the president you found most interesting. Write another page on the president that your parent liked. Make a cover for your report. Be sure you write a rough draft and a final copy. The rough draft must be handed in to the teacher on Wednesday, so he can look it over. The project is due on Friday.

 Next to each day in the schedule below, write what your friend should do.

work schedule for your friend

SAT	_____
SUN	_____
MON	_____
TUES	_____
WED	_____
THUR	_____

How Do You Study Best?

Sometimes where, when, and how you study make a BIG difference in how well you do. Below is a list of study suggestions. If you've already tried some of these different ways to study, rate how they work for you. If they're new ideas, give them a try and see if they're helpful. Then come back to this page and rate them.

Remember to use the ideas that work well for you. It will make things easier and you will see good results. You should also come up with ideas of your own. You may even want to ask your friends how they study to get new techniques.

Study Techniques	Doesn't work for me	Can be somewhat helpful	This is great!
Studying in the morning	☐	☐	☐
Studying in the afternoon	☐	☐	☐
Studying in the evening	☐	☐	☐
Studying by myself	☐	☐	☐
Studying with a friend	☐	☐	☐
Studying with a tutor or parent	☐	☐	☐
Working in a quiet room	☐	☐	☐
Working in a noisy place	☐	☐	☐
Working with quiet music in the background	☐	☐	☐
Studying while I sit at a desk	☐	☐	☐
Studying while I walk around	☐	☐	☐

Study Techniques	Doesn't work for me	Can be somewhat helpful	This is great!
Writing important information down over and over	☐	☐	☐
Reading my notes out loud	☐	☐	☐
Having my parents give me practice tests	☐	☐	☐
Listening to my notes on a tape recorder or a digital voice recorder	☐	☐	☐
Working in an area with bright lights	☐	☐	☐
Working in an area lit by a lamp	☐	☐	☐
Studying when I am tired	☐	☐	☐
Studying when I am wide awake	☐	☐	☐
Studying after I have exercised	☐	☐	☐
Studying while I pet my cat or dog	☐	☐	☐
Studying in the library	☐	☐	☐
Studying outdoors	☐	☐	☐
Studying with other people	☐	☐	☐

Write some of your own ideas here.

_____   _____

_____   _____

_____   _____

More Study Suggestions

Here are some study suggestions that other kids with AD/HD have found helpful. After you've tried them, check the ones you find useful. Add some of your own at the bottom. Talk to your friends and see if they have any suggestions. You might also discuss this page with your teacher, parent, or tutor to get more ideas.

○ If you have a lot of facts to memorize, try saying them into a tape recorder. Then listen to them over and over again on the tape.

○ Make up flash cards (with answers on the back). Study from them. Try cards for spelling and vocabulary words, math facts, history facts, foreign language words, or science questions.

○ Walk around or pedal a stationary bike as you study.

○ If you have to read a whole chapter, try reading one page at a time. When you finish each page, write a sentence or two about the main facts or ideas on that page.

○ Use different colors to underline important ideas in your notes or books.

○ Try drawing a diagram or map to help you understand an idea.

○ Discuss information that will be on the test with someone else (another student in the class, a parent, or a tutor).

○ Have your parents, tutor, or friend make up a practice test for you to take.

Other ideas:

_____

_____

_____

Which three techniques work best for you when studying?

1. _____

2. _____

3. _____

Test Planner

Starting your studying several days before you have a test lets you divide up the work. That way you will feel confident and well prepared.

The next time you have a test use this page as your study helper. Ask an adult to help you the first few times you use it. Try to complete this planner several days before the test.

1. Subject of the test _____

2. Date of the test _____

3. Number of days that you have to study _____

4. What do you need to know for the test? _____

5. How do you plan to study for this test? (Use some ideas from the Study

   Suggestions on page 82.) _____

6. Develop a work schedule using the form below.

work schedule

day	material to study	time scheduled
_____	_____	_____
_____	_____	_____
_____	_____	_____
_____	_____	_____
_____	_____	_____
_____	_____	_____
_____	_____	_____

Test Check-Up

How did you do on your test?

☐ Could do better ☐ Good ☐ Excellent

What type of mistakes did you make on this test?

Examples:

☐ Spent too much time on some questions and not enough on others

☐ Didn't read the directions carefully

☐ Didn't know vocabulary

☐ Didn't know factual information

☐ Didn't check over my work

☐ Didn't write enough on short essays

☐ Didn't finish test

Other _____

Did you feel prepared for the test? _____

If you didn't, why not? _____

_____

What did you do that was most helpful for this test? _____

_____

What study ideas will you try for the next test? _____

_____

 Talk about ways you can avoid mistakes and do better the next time with your teacher, tutor, or counselor. You can use this sheet with all of your tests to follow your progress and see which strategies work for you.

Remembering What You Read

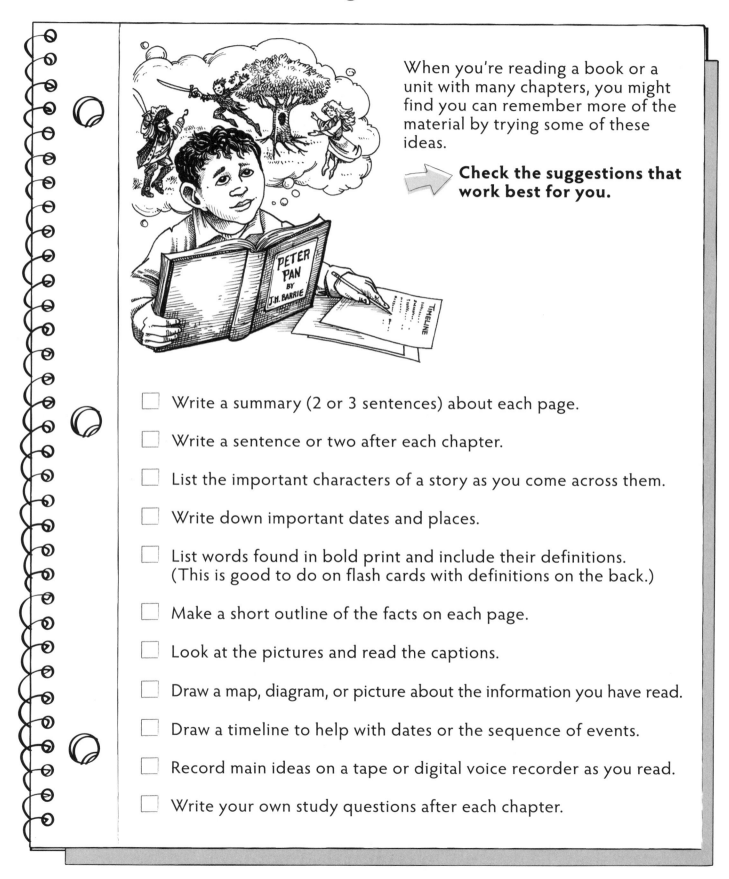

When you're reading a book or a unit with many chapters, you might find you can remember more of the material by trying some of these ideas.

Check the suggestions that work best for you.

☐ Write a summary (2 or 3 sentences) about each page.

☐ Write a sentence or two after each chapter.

☐ List the important characters of a story as you come across them.

☐ Write down important dates and places.

☐ List words found in bold print and include their definitions. (This is good to do on flash cards with definitions on the back.)

☐ Make a short outline of the facts on each page.

☐ Look at the pictures and read the captions.

☐ Draw a map, diagram, or picture about the information you have read.

☐ Draw a timeline to help with dates or the sequence of events.

☐ Record main ideas on a tape or digital voice recorder as you read.

☐ Write your own study questions after each chapter.

Getting the Information

In school you read pages filled with important information. Writing things down helps many people "hold on" to facts better.

 To practice, read these paragraphs. Then follow the directions below.

Do you like to ice skate? Did you know that people in the Scandinavian countries and the Netherlands ice skated about 1,000 years ago? They skated on frozen lakes and rivers. People in cold countries used skates to travel around when it was cold and icy.

In 1592, a man from Scotland invented ice skates that were made of iron. Ice skating was introduced in the United States in the 1740's. In 1814, the first world speed skating race took place in England.

In 1850, blades of steel were made to be used for ice skating. They were put on the bottom of people's boots. About 40 years later, skates were produced with the blades as part of the boots. These skates were created by Jackson Haines, who was an American ballet dancer and figure skater. The first artificial ice rink was built in 1876 in London, England. Today, people all over the world enjoy ice skating both outdoors and at indoor rinks.

Write one or two sentences to summarize each of these paragraphs.

_____

_____

_____

_____

_____

_____

_____

_____

_____

What are some of the important facts in each paragraph?

_____

_____

_____

_____

_____

_____

_____

_____

_____

_____

_____

_____

_____

_____

_____

_____

_____

_____

Draw a timeline of the dates below.

_____ / _____ / _____ / _____ / _____

Organizing Your Writing

A graphic organizer, or web, is another good way to get your ideas organized before you begin writing a paragraph or report. It also is a very useful study guide. Here is an example of a web for a report about Alaska.

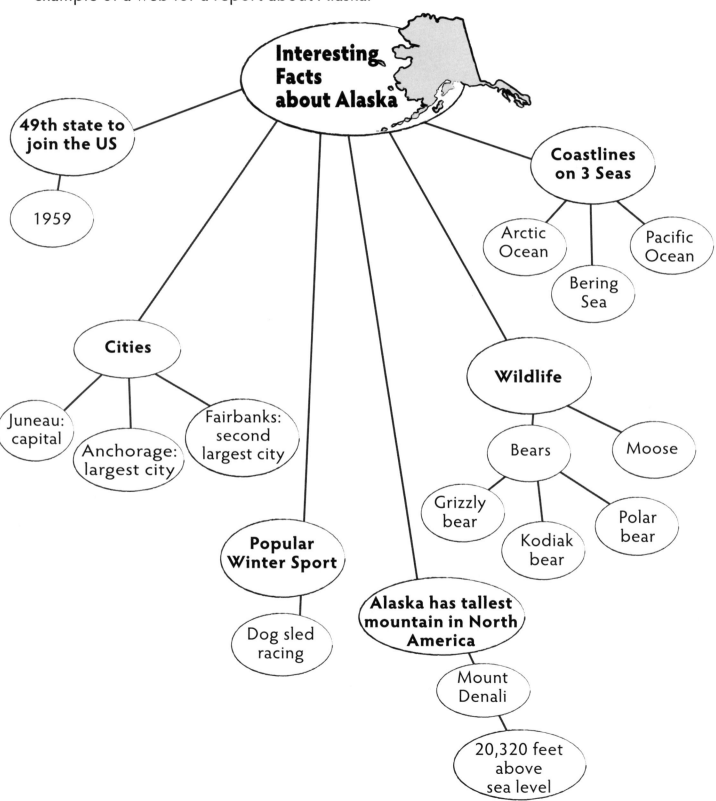

Try making your own web. Look up information on the state of Texas and fill in your information below.

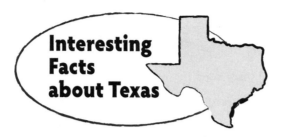

Practice Outlining

Outlining before you write a paragraph or report is a good way to organize your writing. Once you've organized all of your ideas into an outline, it makes it easier to stay organized when you write, give a speech, or follow a plan.

Here is a sample of an organized outline:

House Pets
I. Cats
    A. Very popular pets
    B. Like to climb on high places
    C. Love to play
    D. Keep themselves very clean
II. Dogs
    A. Able to detect scents better than humans can
    B. Can hear high-pitched sounds
    C. Have been pets for thousands of years
    D. Need lots of exercise

 Try making your own outline. Fill in each of the spaces with information.

Equipment Used for Team Sports

I. Baseball

    A. Bats

    B. Bases

    C. _____

    D. _____

II. Soccer

    A. _____

    B. _____

    C. _____

    D. _____

Answers

P 26 Building an AD/HD Support Team

P 30 Exercise Can Be Fun!

Running	Biking
Lacrosse	Wrestling
Jumping rope	Playing catch
Basketball	Building a snowman
Swimming	Karate
Golf	Soccer
Dancing	Field hockey
Tennis	Flying kites

P 31 Playing Outdoors for Exercise

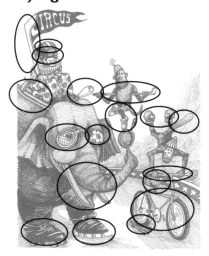

P 33 Finding Your Green Space

1. park
2. backyard
3. playground
4. bike path
5. pond
6. track
7. garden
8. nature trail
9. campground
10. zoo
11. tree house
12. arboretum
13. greenhouse
14. athletic field

P 37 Medication Check-Up

P 41 How Can You Manage Your AD/HD Better?

1. Exercising
2. medicine
3. doctor
4. should
5. An orange
6. focus
7. once a week
8. counselor
9. relax
10. decrease
11. can be

P 50 Organizing Your Room

P 53 Making Your Morning Go Smoothly

P 64 What Do You See?

A. A vase or two faces.

B. Both! This figure is called the Penrose Square. It can be drawn on paper but is impossible to build in three dimensions.

C. A map. Usually we view the water as background for the land. In this map, the black area is the Mediterranean Sea and the white area is Europe and Africa.

D. Both sections are the same. This is called the Muller-Lyer Illusion. This is so strong that it occurs even when there is proof that the distance between arrows is the same, as with this ruler:

P 65 What's Wrong Here?

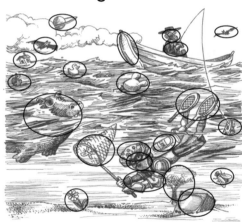

P 66 Look Carefully

1. slip
2. quit
3. since
4. happiest
5. shingle
6. coordinated
7. were
8. chose
9. there
10. hopping
11. flight
12. heartfelt
13. hematosis

P 67 What's the Correct Order?

A. 4, 3, 2, 1
B. 5, 3, 2, 4, 1
C. 2, 5, 4, 3, 1

P 70 Telling the Story

A. 2, 4, 1, 3
B. 2, 4, 3, 1
C. 3, 1, 4, 2

P 71 Finish What You Start

P 72 Try It!

exit   enter

P 76 Correcting Your Work

1. 63
2. 11
3. 67
4. 48
5. 24
6. 72
7. 55
8. 5
9. 269
10. 11,760
11. 93
12. 10

P 77 Proofreading Your Work

Last week, we went to visit my aunt and uncle, who live in Chicago, Illinois. When Aunt Mary saw me, she said in a loud voice, "I can't believe how much you've grown since last year!" We had fun being together. Next year, I hope we can spend more than two days in Chicago.

Glossary

A

Attention Deficit Disorder (ADD). A set of problems that includes difficulty paying attention and focusing. It also includes increased distractibility.

Attention Deficit Hyperactivity Disorder (AD/HD). A condition in a person of average or above-average intelligence that includes symptoms such as short attention span, distractibility, impulsivity, and/or hyperactivity.

B

Brain. The major organ of the nervous system. It controls all mental and physical activities.

Brain Stem. A part of the brain that controls automatic functions such as breathing, heart rate, and blood pressure.

C

Cerebellum. A part of the brain that controls the movements of the muscles, helps with balance, and controls attention.

Cerebral Cortex. The outermost layer of the brain. Its networks are essential to higher thinking activities. It makes up 40% of total brain weight.

Counselor. A professional who works with kids or adults to help them understand feelings and solve their problems. Counselors may work in schools or have offices in other places.

D

Disorder. Something that is not working the way it should.

Disorganization. Difficulty keeping track of materials and/or time.

Distractibility. Trouble staying focused on just one thing.

Dose. The correct amount of medicine a person needs to take at one time for the medicine to work properly.

E

Evaluate. To judge or to look back and check performance.

F

Focusing. Paying careful attention.

H

Hyperactivity. Excessive body movements that are usually without purpose and greater than normally seen at a certain age.

I

Impulsivity. Acting or speaking without thinking

Inattention. Not paying attention.

Irritable. Overly sensitive or in a bad mood.

L

Learning Disabilities. Significant difficulties in learning to read, write, or do mathematics that cause problems in school achievement.

Long-term Assignments. Assignments that are due several days or weeks form the time they are first given.

M

Medication. Substances used to treat illnesses or to improve functioning of the body or brain.

Motivate. To encourage or increase a person's desire to perform a task or learn.

N

Neuron. A single brain cell.

Neurotransmitters. Chemical substances produced by brain cells (neurons) that act as messengers. They cross the space (synapse) between cells and carry information to other brain cells.

O

Organized. Being able to put things in their correct order or place.

P

Pediatrician. A medical doctor who is a specialist in the health of kids and adolescents.

Prescribe. To write direction for the preparation and use of a medicine.

Proofread. To check over written work for errors in spelling, punctuation, capitalization, and grammar.

R

Reminder. A method to help you remember something.

S

Sequencing. Putting things in their correct order.

Side Effects. Uncomfortable reactions that are sometimes caused by medicine.

Stimulant Medications (stimulants). Drugs that increase attention and focus. Stimulants are commonly used to treat AD/HD.

Subcortex. The area below and surrounded by the cerebral cortex.

Summarize. To briefly state the main idea.

Support. A kind of help given by someone else.

Synapse. An extremely small space between two brain cells (neurons) that can be seen only with a microscope. Neurons send messages to each other across synapses.

T

Therapist. A professional who works with kids or adults to solve problems, understand feelings, or change behavior. A therapist can be a psychologist, counselor, social worker, or psychiatrist.

Tutor. A person who works with kids outside of class to help them learn to do better in school. A tutor may help with a particular subject area, such as math, or learning in general. Tutors can also help kids improve their organization and study skills.

V

Visualize. To picture something in your mind.

Resources for Kids

books

To Learn More about AD/HD

Putting on the Brakes, Third Edition: Understanding and Taking Control of Your ADD or ADHD by Patricia O. Quinn and Judith M. Stern (Magination Press)

Attention, Girls! A Guide to Learn All About Your AD/HD by Patricia O. Quinn (Magination Press)

Learning to Slow Down and Pay Attention, Third Edition by Kathleen Nadeau and Ellen Dixon (Magination Press)

50 Activities and Games for Kids with ADHD by Patricia O. Quinn and Judith M. Stern (Magination Press)

Distant Drums, Different Drummers by Barbara Ingersoll (Cape Publications)

Making the Grade: An Adolescent's Struggle with Attention Deficit Disorder by Roberta Parker and Harvey Parker (Impact Publications)

To Read about Kids with AD/HD

Otto Learns About His Medicine: A Story About Medication for Children with ADHD, Third Edition by Matthew Galvin (Magination Press)

Cory Stories: A Kid's Book About Living with ADHD by Jeanne Kraus (Magination Press)

Sparky's Excellent Misadventures: My A.D.D. Journal, By Me (Sparky) by Phyllis Carpenter and Marti Ford (Magination Press)

Jumpin' Johnny Get Back to Work: A Child's Guide to ADHD/Hyperactivity by Michael Gordon (GSI Publications)

The Adventures of Phoebe Flower by Barbara Roberts (Advantage Books)

Joey Pigza Swallowed a Key by Jack Gantos (HarperTrophy)

Ethan Has Too Much Energy: An Emotional Literacy Book by Lawrence Shapiro (Boulden Publishing)

To Help with Feelings and Behaviors

What-to-Do Guides for Kids by Dawn Huebner, PhD (Magination Press)

> *What to Do When You Worry Too Much: A Kid's Guide to Overcoming Anxiety*
>
> *What to Do When You Grumble Too Much: A Kid's Guide to Overcoming Negativity*
>
> *What to Do When Your Temper Flares: A Kid's Guide to Overcoming Problems with Anger*
>
> *What to Do When You Dread Your Bed: A Kid's Guide to Overcoming Problems with Sleep*

The Behavior Survival Guide for Kids: How to Make Good Choices and Stay Out of Trouble by Thomas McIntyre (Free Spirit Publishing)

To Help You Do Better in School

Annie's Plan: Taking Charge of Schoolwork and Homework by Jeanne Kraus (Magination Press)

Get Organized without Losing It by Janet Fox (Free Spirit Publishing)

How to Do Homework without Throwing Up by Trevor Romain (Free Spirit Publishing)

The Survival Guide for Kids with LD (Learning Differences) (Revised and Updated) by Rhonda Cummings and Gary Fisher (Free Spirit Publishing)

How to Be School Smart: Super Study Skills, Revised Edition by Elizabeth James and Carol Barkin (Beech Tree Books)

games

To Help with Feelings and Behaviors

The Impulse Control Game™
by Franklin Rubenstein (Boulden Publishing)
Ages 7-13 (grades 2-7)

The Self-Control Patrol Game
by Berthold Berg (Childswork/Childsplay)
Ages 8-14 (Grades 3-8)

The Stop, Relax, and Think Game
by the Center for Applied Psychology
(Childswork/Childsplay)
Ages 6-12 (grades 1-6)

To Help You Do Better in School

Following Directions: Taxi Driver
by Learning Well® (Edupress)
Ages 7-13 (grades 2-7)

software for graphic organizers

Kispiration®

(grades K-5)
by Inspiration Software, Inc.

9400 SW Beaverton-Hillsdale Highway, Suite 300
Beaverton, OR 97005-3300

phone: (503) 297-3004
www.inspiration.com

Draft:Builder

(grades 3-12)
by Don Johnston, Inc.

26799 West Commerce Drive
Volo, IL 60073

phone: (847) 740-0749
www.donjohnston.com

organizational materials

Organizational Tools for Students in Grades 3-12

This catalog of useful materials for students contains items
such as structured assignment notebooks and calendars.

To order contact:
Success by Design, Inc.
3741 Linden Avenue
Wyoming, MI 49548

phone: (800) 327-0057
www.successbydesign.com